Pirate Life

By Michael Teitelbaum

The Child's World®
www.childsworld.com

Published in the United States of America by The Child's World®
1980 Lookout Drive • Mankato, MN 56003-1705
800-599-READ • www.childsworld.com

ACKNOWLEDGMENTS

The Child's World® : Mary Berendes, Publishing Director

Produced by Shoreline Publishing Group LLC
President / Editorial Director: James Buckley, Jr.
Designer: Tom Carling, carlingdesign.com
Cover Design: Slimfilms

Photo Credits
Cover–dreamstime.com
Interior–Corbis: 5, 6, 11, 12, 13; dreamstime.com: 8, 16, 20, 22, 23, 25, 26, 28; North Wind Picture Archives: 14, 22; Photos.com: 19 (3), 22 top, 26 bottom.

LIBRARY OF CONGRESS CATALOG-IN-PUBLICATION DATA

Teitelbaum, Michael.
  Pirate life / by Michael Teitelbaum.
     p. cm.
  Includes index.
  ISBN-13: 978-1-59296-859-6 (library bound : alk. paper)
  ISBN-10: 1-59296-859-7 (library bound : alk. paper)
 1. Pirates—Caribbean Area—Juvenile literature. 2. Buccaneers—Juvenile literature. I. Title.

  F2161.T45 2007
  972.9—dc22

                                        2007004203

CONTENTS

HERE THERE BE Pirates!

A skull-and-bones flag flaps in the breeze. Cannons are loaded. A scallywag in an eye patch paces on deck. He waves a sword into the air and shouts a theatening "Arrr!" Shiver me timbers, that can only mean one thing—here there be pirates, matey!

But what is a pirate? Well, they're not really very nice people, actually. Pirates are thieves who rob ships at sea. Some do it just for their own profit. Others are hired by a country to rob its enemies.

We've all seen pirates in movies and books. Thanks to a popular series of movies, more people are talking about pirates than ever. In movies and books, pirates sail the open seas, singing and laughing and fighting. It looks like they're having a pretty good time. But what is pirate life really like? Let's find out!

According to legend, pirates often made their prisoners "walk the plank" before plunging into the raging sea.

Pirates have been around for more than 3,000 years. They **terrorized** the waters of ancient Greece and Rome. Viking pirates traveled the waters of northern Europe. They robbed ships and local villages.

But when most people think of pirates, they think about the Golden Age of Pirates during the 1600s and

Powered by sails and oars, dragon-headed Viking pirate ships were feared in the North Atlantic Ocean.

1700s. Pirates from many nations attacked ships in the Mediterranean and Caribbean Seas.

At that time, Spain had many **colonies** in North and South America. These colonies were rich in gold and treasures. So French, Dutch, and British pirates swooped down on Spanish ships.

Colonies are areas of land owned or controlled by a country in a different part of the world. Spain's colonies, for example, included some Caribbean islands and the area that is now Florida.

This is a modern re-creation of one of the Spanish ships that pirates attacked in search of gold.

It wasn't always just gold that pirates took from the ships. They also kidnapped sailors and passengers. Those prisoners who were rich enough to pay a **ransom** were freed. Those that couldn't pay were put to work rowing the oars of the pirate ship. (We told you they were not very nice guys!)

Pirates called **privateers** were hired by governments to attack their enemies. "Corsairs" terrorized the Mediterranean Sea and the coast of North Africa. "Buccaneers" lived on Caribbean islands.

Over the years, writers, artists, and filmmakers have brought the legends of pirates to life. These storytellers told of horrible raids and thrilling high-sea adventures. Some stories were invented. Others, however, are based on facts. Here are real stories of some of the pirates from the Golden Age of Pirates.

The most famous pirate ever was the Englishman known as Blackbeard. Blackbeard's real name was probably Edward Teach. In the early 1700s, Blackbeard terrorized the Caribbean. He had a thick black beard and long black hair, which he braided and tied with ribbons. He also tied **fuses** into his hair, which he lit during battle so thick smoke swirled around his head.

A Little Privateer Help

Before the American Revolution, the British colonies didn't mind having some pirates in their waters. As long as the pirates attacked Spanish ships, then spent the Spanish gold in the colonies! During the American Revolution, many privateers were hired to fight against the British Royal Navy. In fact, the number of privateers' ships outnumbered the ships in the American Continental Navy eleven to one!

Blackbeard strapped knives, swords, and pistols to his body. He was a very mean pirate. Many ships fled from him in terror.

This painting shows Blackbeard battling with the British sailors who captured him.

In 1718, the British Royal Navy finally succeeded in finding and battling against Blackbeard . . . and they won. The sailors cut off Blackbeard's head.

Sir Francis Drake moved from capturing enemy ships to capturing his countrymen's imagination with his great explorations.

In 1567, Sir Francis Drake, an English admiral, was attacked and defeated by Spanish ships. He spent the next four years as a pirate taking his revenge on the Spanish. He was then hired by Queen Elizabeth to work for England as a privateer. Drake later became the first person to sail around the world.

Welsh pirate Captain Henry Morgan attacked Spain's Caribbean colonies in the 1600s. In 1655 he took Jamaica from the Spanish. In 1670, he raided and captured all of Panama.

A pirate known as the Black Monk raided the English Channel. It was said that he made a deal with the devil so could turn his ship invisible. He was caught in 1217.

This modern ship was designed to look like Drake's famous Golden Hind sailing ship.

This picture shows Captain Kidd in a classic pirate scene—burying treasure on a deserted island.

Born in Scotland, William Kidd became a wealthy **merchant** in New York. Having once worked as a privateer, Captain Kidd was hired by the governor of Massachusetts to capture the pirate Blackbeard. But Captain Kidd had other ideas. He quickly changed sides and became a pirate himself.

Pirate Captain Jean Lafitte attacked British, American, and Spanish ships in the Gulf of Mexico near New Orleans. He was called a pirate and **condemned** to death. But he was also called a hero by many for his bravery fighting against the British in the Battle of New Orleans. His pirates joined Americans to help win that battle during the War of 1812.

Women Pirates

Women weren't usually allowed on pirate ships. So a few women dressed up like men to become pirates. The most famous were Anne Bonny and Mary Read. They sailed together on the pirate ship run by "Calico" Jack Rackham. Both women took part in many attacks and fought as fiercely as the men on board their pirate ship.

2

GET ON BOARD, Matey!

Think you would have made a good pirate? You'd have had to be strong, a good sailor, skilled with a sword, and **ruthless**. Pirate ships were filled with danger. Not to mention terrible food, filthy living conditions, and a bunch of thieves and cutthroat killers who just happened to be your crewmates!

Pirate tales focus on the adventure and treasure. But life on board a pirate ship was often difficult and boring. Everyone worked hard. The ship needed constant repair. The deck and sails had to be patched up. Hot lead had to be formed into cannonballs. Water had to be bailed out. And rats—yes, rats—had to be caught and tossed overboard.

OPPOSITE PAGE
Here's a modern view of the type of ship often used by pirates.

Food also had to be prepared for the crew. Pirates brought chickens on board for eggs and meat. They also caught fish from the sea. And they ate roasted sea-turtle meat. But all this food spoiled on long journeys, so sometimes the meat was combined with lots of spices to hide the rotten taste.

When the fresh food ran out, pirates turned to eating dried beans, salted meats, and rock-hard biscuits called **hardtack**. Also, food stored for a long time was often filled with bugs or nibbled on by rats. Yuck!

It was tough to get fresh drinking water at sea, so pirates drank lots of bottled **ale** and **rum**.

Pirate-to-English Glossary

Here are some handy pirate words to use when you want to talk like a pirate.

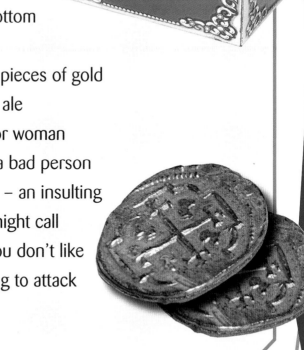

Ahoy – hello

Aye – yes

Booty – treasure

Davy Jones' Locker – the bottom of the ocean

Doubloons – pieces of gold

Grog – pirate ale

Lass – a girl or woman

Scallywag – a bad person

Scurvy Dog – an insulting name you might call someone you don't like

Swaggy – a ship you're going to attack

Thar – there

Yo-ho-ho – Pirate laughter

No, it's not the guy from the movies! But this costume shows many things pirate leaders wore: leather boots, pistol belts, tri-corner hats, and jewelry.

If you were a pirate, you'd wash in rainwater or in the sea. You'd also wear just one set of clothing. Most pirates wore baggy shirts, no shoes, and thick canvas pants covered with tar to keep out the water. And pirates smelled really awful!

If a pirate was wearing fine clothes, it meant he stole them! The captain got first choice of stolen velvet jackets, fancy hats, buckled shoes, or fine leather straps for holding his weapons.

Talk Like a Pirate

Did you know that September 19th is Talk Like a Pirate Day? Here are some tips to get you ready.

1) Always speak in the present tense. Instead of saying "I am," say "I be." Instead of saying "my," say "me," as in "That be me sword."

2) Never pronounce the letter "G" at the end of words. Instead of saying "fighting" or "swimming," say "fightin'" or "swimmin'."

3) Don't call your friends "Pal" or "Bud" or "Dude." Instead, call them "Matey" or "Me hearty."

4) Start each sentence with a loud "Arrr!" Here's a good sample pirate sentence: "Arrrr! That be me ship you be shootin' at, matey!"

Pirates used compasses, telescopes, maps, and charts to find their way. Pirate ships also flew flags that announced their intentions to attack other ships.

Most of a pirate's time was taken up by hard work, but they did have some time for fun. They would sing songs, dance, draw pictures, and even give each other tattoos.

A good telescope and a treasure map were very useful to pirates.

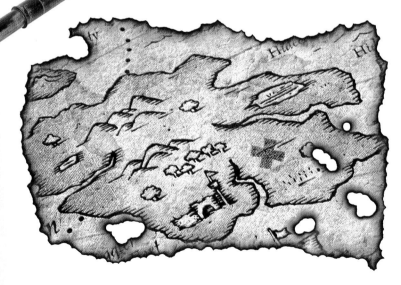

The most famous pirate flags featured this design of a skull and crossed bones. The design was known as the "Jolly Roger."

Although they were thieves and murderers, pirates lived by their own strict code. This told them how to behave, how all treasure was to be divided up, and how to punish a scallywag who cheated his mates. Pirate punishments included being marooned, which means being left alone on a deserted island!

So, even with the bad food, the long hours, and the smell, still think you would have liked being a pirate?

Attack!

Imagine that you're a long-ago pirate. You've spotted a ship. It looks like a rich merchant vessel. It could be filled with cloth, spices, animals, rum, sugar, flour, wood, copper, jewels, silk, medicine, and, of course, silver and gold! What are you going to do now? Attack, of course!

The merchant ship has spotted the skull and crossbones on your flag. It begins to flee. But it can't outrun your swift pirate ship. When you're close enough, you fire your cannon.

Large iron cannons such as this one would shoot heavy cannonballs from the pirate ships to their targets.

A chain-shot—two cannonballs linked by a metal chain—rips into the merchant ship's main sail. Its **mast** comes crashing to its deck. The ship can no longer sail. It sits still in the water. Now you board!

You leap from your ship onto theirs, waving your cutlass sword, firing your pistol, and screaming threats at the top of your lungs. You light the fuse of your grenade.

Pirate Weapons

Cutlass – a pirate's sword. It had a short blade to stop it from getting tangled up in a ship's ropes.

Flintlock Pistol – a small, light gun that was easy to carry when boarding a ship. It took so long to reload, though, that after one shot, pirates just used the gun as a club.

Boarding Ax – this long-handled ax was used to cut through ropes and wood. It was also used as a hook to help pirates climb up the sides of ships.

Chain-shot – two cannonballs linked together by a metal chain.

Grenade – a clay pot that could be filled with gunpowder to explode, or with tar and rags to create a smokescreen while boarding a ship.

It's a clay pot filled with gunpowder. You toss it onto the deck and— BOOM!—it explodes everywhere.

Most crews don't even put up a fight. Those foolish enough to fight you meet a quick death by your sword, ax, or pistol. The ship is now yours. Now you can loot the booty!

You take whatever is of value. And sometimes you even take the ship. If the ship you raid is in better shape than the one you came on, you move onto that ship. If your ship is still in good shape, you take the other ship and split your crew.

Its sails rolled up for a port visit, a three-masted ship sits in the glow of sunset.

Pirate Superstitions

Pirates were a superstitious bunch. Here are some of the things they believed:

1) Black bags on a pirate ship brought bad luck.
2) Starting a voyage on a Friday brought bad luck.
3) Women on a pirate ship brought bad luck.
4) Porpoises near a ship brought good luck.
5) If a bucket or mop fell overboard, it was bad luck.
6) Tattooing an open eye on each of a pirate's eyelids was thought to help him see while he slept.

Now you have two ships sailing the seas in search of booty.

For a pirate, the life was hard, but the rewards could be great. Death and danger lurked around each bend. But so did excitement, adventure, and the promise of unimaginable treasure.

GLOSSARY

ale a brewed alcoholic drink

colonies areas of land controlled by a faraway country

condemned sentenced

fuses thin pieces of rope that carry gunpowder to shoot a cannon or explode a grenade

hardtack biscuits pirates ate during long sea journeys

mast the tall pole on a ship that holds the sail

merchant someone who makes a living selling things

privateers pirates hired by a country to attack enemies of that country on the sea

ransom money demanded for the release of a kidnapped person

rum an alcoholic drink made from molasses

ruthless without any remorse for doing something wrong

superstitions acts or things believed to bring good or bad luck

terrorized threatened, frightened, or attacked

FIND OUT MORE

BOOKS

The Best Book of Pirates
By Barnaby Howard (Kingfisher, 2006)
Everything you wanted to know about pirates.

Pirates
By John Matthews (Atheneum, 2006)
All about pirate history and life on board pirate ships.

Pirates
By Greg Nickles (Crabtree, 1997)
Great pirate facts and myths.

WEB SITES

Visit our Web page for lots of links about pirates and their world:
www.childsworld.com/links

Note to Parents, Teachers, and Librarians: We routinely check our Web links to make sure they're safe, active sites—so encourage your readers to check them out!

INDEX

MICHAEL TEITELBAUM has never been a pirate, but he has been a writer, editor, and packager of children's books, comic books, and magazines for more than 25 years. He wrote *Making Comic Books* and *Famous Ghosts* for the Reading Rocks! series. Michael has also written books based on comic-book characters such as Superman, Batman, Spider-Man, and Garfield. He also created and edited *Spider-Man Magazine* for Marvel Comics. Michael and his wife, Sheleigah, live in New York City.